REASON FOR THE FOUNDING OF THE SCHOOL

Barhadbshabba

Bishop of Hulwan

Translated by: Addai Scher, D.P. Curtin

REASON FOR THE FOUNDING OF THE SCHOOL

Copyright @ 2020 Dalcassian Press

All rights reserved. No part of this publication may be reproduced, distributed, or transmitted in any form or by any means, including photocopying, recording, or other electronic or mechanical methods, without the prior written permission of the publisher, except in the case of brief quotations embodied in critical reviews and certain other non-commercial uses permitted by copyright law. For permission request, write to Dalcassian Press at dalcassianpublishing at gmail.com

ISBN: 979-8-3302-6689-0 (Paperback)

Library of Congress Control Number:
Author: Curtin, D.P. (1985-)

Printed by Ingram Content Group, 1 Ingram Blvd, La Vergne, Tennessee

First printing edition 2020.

REASON FOR THE FOUNDING OF THE SCHOOL

REASON FOR THE FOUNDING OF THE SCHOOL

REASON FOR THE FOUNDING OF THE SCHOOL

Skillful architects, in laying the foundations of a building, place a solid stone that fits into the entire construction and can support it. Similarly, for skillful architects of the fear of God, the first stone of their word in the construction of their monument must be a testimony of gratitude for the goodness of the Creator. The second foundation, after the first, is his unfathomable wisdom; and the third, his invincible power. Whoever possesses these three qualities will have no obstacles in his works. The nature of reasonable beings, although endowed with the greatness of grace, cannot possess these qualities in their integrity and even what she promises is not without alloy, for her goodness, because it is accidental, is hindered by evil; her wisdom, because it is acquired, is opposed by ignorance; her strength, because it is weak and temporary, is hindered by weakness. It is necessary indeed that the fruits correspond to the tree itself, that the properties of nature correspond to what nature itself is, and that temporary things are what time is, variable itself. Therefore, what she promises (the nature of beings endowed with reason) can only be subject to changes and variations.

As for the Creator of times and variations, none of our weaknesses can hinder him. His goodness is recognized by this sign that it is not us who prayed for him to create us, according to the testimony of Scripture which says: The world will be built by goodness'; and the earth is filled with the goodness of the Lord; and also Lord! the earth is full of your grace. The similar texts that manifest the Lord's goodness towards us are countless.

As for his inscrutable wisdom, the blessed Paul, this chosen vessel, says with admiration: O depth of the riches and wisdom and knowledge of God! He alone is wise; it is he who grants wisdom to the wise and knowledge to those who have understanding; who has been his counselor?

As for the greatness of his invincible power, who could say that anything could resist him? It is the Lord who made the earth by his power; he gives strength to those who are weak. Who is like you, Almighty God? There are many other texts that reveal his invincible

REASON FOR THE FOUNDING OF THE SCHOOL

power to us. Now, three things prevent the nature of beings endowed with reason and created to do good, they are evil, ignorance, and weakness.

However, as we have just demonstrated through the holy books, none of these obstacles exist for God. Let us therefore carefully consider the attributes of God and cast away from our thoughts anything that might afflict us; let us consider that God created us out of his kindness, without us having asked, and that by his wisdom, he has ensured that we have a double life: a mortal life suitable for the needy and those called to learn, and a life of the perfect suitable for the happiness of the righteous. But by his kindness, he wanted, by his wisdom, he administered, and by his power, he perfected. And the proof of God's works, we take it from this world just as he created us. He will raise us up by his grace, and by his wisdom He will transport us from here to heaven, and this power, which nothing can hinder in our first education, will have no obstacles in our second instruction (regeneration). Therefore, with sound knowledge and right reason, we must consider the works of God and consider of great interest all that is due to his action.

Because of the weakness of my body, which constantly languishes in pains and various illnesses, I could not speak to you even for a single day. But God, who knows your dedication and love for him, you who have forsaken your countries, your parents, and, in short, have despised the pleasures of this world to love and cherish only this spiritual occupation, which enlightens souls and serves as salt for those who have lost the taste for truth and heavenly food, you who have chosen exile, suffering, pain, deprivation, fatigue, labor, vigilance, and diligent study of divine books over everything else, God, I say, has strengthened and helped me by his grace. Not that I was worthy of it, but so that you may not remain idle, so that your efforts may not be in vain. Indeed, it is the habit of divine grace to act.

So; it is still she who is the cause of the formation of the world and of our first creation. For no one prayed to God to create creatures, except by His grace and mercy. He showed and manifested His grace more by His words towards us, by the honor He gave us to govern us, by His care for us, and by the forgiveness of our faults and sins. Although we have been constantly ungrateful and sinners, by His patience, He has sustained us with life-giving laws, which, from century to century,

REASON FOR THE FOUNDING OF THE SCHOOL

have been established for our benefit, especially by the law, which, through the blessed Moses, was given to the people of Israel, so that they could acquire the love of God and the love of neighbor, that they might turn away from the worship of idols and recognize the one who is the only true and eternal God.

After all these things, as a crowning blessing, we have had this glorious and ineffable gift, namely the coming of Christ, through whose hands all the riches of His goodness and immeasurable mercy have been poured out on us. Although all these graces are common to all believers, however, it is you who enjoy them the most, because you study and meditate on them and because they are a delight and an excellent reward for you, more than any kind of wealth.

You know indeed the origin of this institution, what were the causes that led to its suppression in Edessa and its foundation in this city by Mar Bar-Sauma, bishop, and by Rabban Mar Narsaï, priest, virtuous and divine men, and how, after their death, not only did it not fall into decline and ruin, because God enlarged it and made it prosper even more, despite the agitations and troubles stirred up against it, from time to time, by the operation of Satan. Significant benefits resulted from it for the Persian kingdom, as evidenced by the institutions that emerged from it and that now exist in several places; for all these graces, we cannot thank God enough for making us worthy of such favors. What care He has for us, who are unworthy of it! Therefore, we pray to God to preserve (this school), to maintain it, and to strengthen it eternally.

You too must strive to apply yourselves to work, to observe, and to benefit from the regulations prescribed to you and passed down to you by your predecessors, so that you too may pass on these goods and advantages to those who will succeed you.

As for God, created beings speak of Him in two ways: either by saying what He is in Himself, or by attributing to Him what is inferior to Him. But we cannot apply to Him anything that is above His nature. For if we say that He is the eternal being, the infinite Spirit, the Cause of all things, we are defining Him according to His own nature. If, on the contrary, we say that He is composed, corporeal, devoid of knowledge, and needy, we are applying to Him things that are below the order and outside of correctness.

REASON FOR THE FOUNDING OF THE SCHOOL

Indeed, although the word "being" is common to all beings and also to a single being, it is only to God that it accurately and exactly applies: because everything that exists is either created or uncreated; now, just as concerning the created being, the word "being" is prior to the word "is" and the former is the cause of the latter, so too, concerning the uncreated being, the word "eternal being" is prior to the word "is," and it is the former that is the cause of the latter. For if it exists and is not an eternal being, then it is created; now, if this is true, it has a beginning, and it owes its existence to another; and thus, it would be equal to all beings in these two states, as it was created and as it is. Therefore, if this hypothesis, understood in this way, is absurd, God is because He is the Being; and the creature is because it was created and had a beginning.

It is unquestionably certain that there is only one being who is, from the beginning, before all beings. It can even be said that not only (the phrase): being alone before all beings, but even the words 'in principio' do not suit him. For all these terms are used only by analogy. God, being from all eternity, has neither name nor appellation; he is above all designation. He was not made, and had no beginning; for these words: to exist, to begin were not yet known, except in the knowledge (divine) that penetrates everything. He alone was from all eternity; he enjoyed, as now, a happy essence; he dwelt in a resplendent light, in an indescribable and unfathomable manner. But he knew himself, and he was known by himself in himself and from himself as now. But it is impossible for rational beings to say and even to think in what manner God knew himself: No one knows the Son, says Jesus Christ, except the Father, and no one knows the Father except the Son. Saint Paul also testifies: Who knows what is in man, except the spirit of man that is in him? Likewise, no one knows what is in God, except the Spirit of God.

God, existing in His own attributes, in an inexpressible way, thought cannot grasp this divine essence, with which time that begins with movement and movement that is inherent to the essence, are incompatible. It is the depth of depths, unfathomable and unfindable. Thought has no path to walk to this divine majesty that is above the paths and practicable paths of thought, this agile steed of the soul. Since thought has no path to walk on, speech itself, a swift four-footed steed, falters and is forced to interrupt its walk because the acuity of thought, which is the guide and mistress of speech, being dazzled and blinded, becomes unable to contemplate this majestic light, unless Our Lord, in His kindness, grants us the grace to reveal and make known to us His nature, even if only in an elementary way, as Saint Paul says: The knowledge of God has been revealed to them; and, showing how this knowledge has been revealed, he adds: it is God who has revealed it to them and to us, God has revealed it to us through His Spirit. And Our Lord said: [No one knows the Father except the Son] and the one to whom the Son wills to make Him known. I have manifested your name to men. Otherwise, this very fragment of knowledge could never fix its gaze on the divine essence. For what is proper to it is ineffably inaccessible to the thought and speech of creatures.

Even knowing that we know nothing escapes, I believe, knowledge. Indeed, one who asserts that they have understood the unknowable is inferior to a stillborn child: for they are in absolute ignorance; if they acknowledge God as unknowable, they will be acknowledged by God himself as wise. With the divine essence being thus, let us see how we can learn to know it and what the difference is between creatures and their Creator.

Although the word creature is a universal term, it nevertheless contains several kinds and several species. Just as the words spirit, body, nature, being, although they apparently have only one appellation, this name, however, applies to several beings and to each of these beings that are distinct and do not resemble each other, that are different and do not agree, so the word created, though unique, implies in its meaning other names. Because everything that exists is either substance (ousia) or accident; each of these two divisions (substance and accident) has its own nature. They are subdivided into other species (modes) that result from them. Thus, every substance is material or immaterial.

Furthermore, matter is divided into several other subdivisions that it implies, namely: into animate and inanimate matter, sensitive and devoid of sensitivity. Likewise, animate matter is further divided into other divisions into living matter and matter devoid of life, into mobile matter and devoid of movement. Moreover, what is alive and moves is subdivided into other distinctions that are subordinate to it, that is, into reasonable and unreasonable; reasonable substances themselves into spiritual or animate; and unreasonable substances into vital or

REASON FOR THE FOUNDING OF THE SCHOOL

non-vital. The spiritual being is divided into finite and infinite, eternal and temporal, and into the one who is the cause of everything or the effect of the cause of everything, which is God.

The excellence of a being does not consist in the fact that it exists, but in what it is and in its way of being; for the former is universal, the latter is individual. Thus, the ox is more perfect than the stone, not because of its size, but because it is alive and sensitive; the king and the priest surpass (the people), not as men, but because of their dignity and the honor due to them. The angel is above man and his immortality; and God is superior to his creatures by his essence and his eternity, which is his own. As for the fact of existence, it is common to him and to us. And just as man is more perfect than all bodies, not as corporeal, but as rational; and the angel is more perfect than all corporeal beings, not because he is not corporeal, but because he is living and immortal; so God is superior to all, not in that he exists, but in his way of being.

Despite this, however great God may be in his nature, however high he may be in his majesty, and distinct from other beings, He has accepted, for our instruction, that we speak of him according to the concrete language of creatures. In science itself, we find that lower distinctions take the name of superior beings; but superior beings do not take the name of lower beings. Thus, man is a living and rational being by his essence; now everything that lives, like animals, poultry, and insects, is not man; likewise, not everything that lives is animal, like plants; not everything that is nature, like stone and raw matter, is animated; likewise, not all those who are of nature are corporeal, like angels and souls.

But, although all beings fall into these divisions, however, the science concerning the Creator and the creature is found only in these two categories, that is to say, in angels and men. But as we are too weak to fix our gaze on this divine essence, God placed in us an invisible lamp, which is our soul; he filled it with the oil of immortal life; he provided it with the multiple wicks which are the thoughts endowed with knowledge; he spread in it the light of divine intelligence, by which we can see and distinguish, like that woman who had lost one of her ten drachmas, the hidden works of the Creator, and explore the rich treasure of his kingdom, until we find, ourselves, that drachma imprinted with the august image of the eternal King of kings. (This is what we could never do), without this divine light, as Saint John says: 'In Him was life, and the life was the light of men', namely the intellectual force, as Our Lord says 'If the light within you is darkness, how great is that darkness; if a blind man leads a blind man, both will fall into a pit'. That is why he commands us, saying 'Walk while

You have the light of reason, in divine wisdom, lest the darkness of error and ignorance surprise you.
This reasonable and enlightened intelligence, which is the image of its Creator, has had the privilege of dwelling in two places: a part dwells on this earth, where it is clothed in the corporeal robe, and where it conducts itself in the fold of flesh; and the other part has had the privilege of walking up there in the fluid plain of the air (*apr*) these are all spiritual beings (*tágma*).

But as our word concerns the intelligence that is in us, let us see how it is in us and what its seat is. The Greek philosophers were so mistaken that they even attributed to it the name of divinity. Its principle and reason for being is the soul that is bound in us and has three intellectual faculties, namely: the mind (*mens*), the sense (*internal*), and the thought. From these three faculties arise three others, which are: desire, anger, and will. Intelligence is above all these faculties, like a wise coachman (*aniochos*) and a skillful pilot (*kubernetas*), whose regard plunges into the distance and steers its boat loaded with treasures away from the rocks of error and the storms of ignorance; through the first intellectual faculties, it refines the cognitive forces of the soul so that they do not mistake one thing for another, but rather grasp the truth and certainty of objects; through the other practical part, it purifies the animal forces of the soul, predisposing them in such a way that they do not behave in vain but that their movements are in line with equity and propriety.

However, since the faculties over which it rules are diverse and different from each other, in order not to shipwreck because of their diversity and not to perish because of their contrasts, intelligence provided, like a swimmer on the waves of the sea, as a skin and boat, the new ship of reasoning, so that through it she could walk without fear on the surface of the world, and in terms of pearls and precious stones, she could draw from it the wisdom of the fear of God, which is acquired through right knowledge.

REASON FOR THE FOUNDING OF THE SCHOOL

And, since everything contained in science is divided into two parts, namely theory and practice, it must be known that the perfection of the theory consists of grasping and understanding exactly all beings, and that the perfection of practice is the excellence of goods (good actions).

And since theory and practice each have their opposite, as shadow has the body as its opposite, and accident has substance as its opposite, that is to say, as a complement to theory and substance, the necessity of reasoning imposed itself as a means to help us distinguish this opposition from the complete perfection of each of the faculties of the soul. Indeed, if the perfect complement of theory is the exact knowledge of all existing things, it is clear that ignorance is its opposite. Thus, we need reasoning to distinguish truth from falsehood; for what is revealed as true, we grasp through a healthy conviction based on knowledge of things; and what is recognized as false by the testimony of truthful arguments, we abandon as contrary to the truth. It is therefore evident that without reason, it cannot be properly distinguished and known by those who judge the objects humanely. For one who does not speak by the Spirit of God, his doctrine, to be believed by the listeners, needs evidence based on reason.

The same is true of this second part, which is practice. Because if its perfection consists in the choice of good actions, as we have shown, it is clear that the opposite of good is evil. In this part too, we need reasoning to distinguish between good and evil, lest in pursuing good, we choose evil without knowing it and abandon good. Indeed, no one deliberately exalts evil and blames good. What is shown by this art as good is truly good; and what is shown as evil must necessarily be truly evil.

Through this admirable instrument of reasoning, intelligence draws all the august images of certain knowledge; it erects a glorious statue according to the original type. So that the theory and reasoning of intelligence do not remain inactive and useless - because it did not have an alphabet to construct names and spell, to learn about this (*divine*) essence and manifest the power of this majesty, it was necessary for the exercise of its faculties and as a sign of its freedom, that its Creator made this corporeity, adorned it with forces and colors, divided it into kinds and species, distinguished it by figures. The operations, granted her individual properties, and placed her in

REASON FOR THE FOUNDING OF THE SCHOOL

that vast interval which is between heaven and earth. He arranged and wrote, so to speak, on a table, all visible bodies, so that intelligence may read therein, and may know through them the author of this teaching - as Paul says: They ask God and seek Him, and it is in His works that they find Him, so that he may possess excellent goods, enjoy His admirable beauties and place upon his head a crown of joy, adorned with the beauties and praises of this excellent Master.

The noble creatures, which are invisible, dwell in the upper spaces and vast regions of the firmament: This man Gabriel, as Daniel says, whom I had seen in vision before, swiftly flew down from heaven. Our Lord said to the Jews: From now on you will see the heavens opened, and the angels of God ascending and descending upon the Son of Man. The ladder of Jacob also demonstrates the existence of angels, who have the power to cultivate this immense plain of the air, from top to bottom, operating useful and fortifying changes therein: They are powerful in strength, it is said, and carry out His orders, and are His ministers who execute His will.

But so that this lower part does not grieve and does not envy the glory of the upper part, its companion, God honored it with the name of his image and likeness, and granted it the name of his divinity: I have said, it is written you are gods and you are all children of the Most High'. He gave (to man) the strength to ascend to heaven and the lofty vaults; and there, as in the palace (palation) of the kingdom and in the celestial vestibules, he travels all the paths and vast streets that are above the higher heavens. Sometimes, to recreate himself, he descends into the spacious interval of the firmament and the sky, as if he were alone in a royal palace. He springs from there, when he wants, to this earthly place, which is below the firmament. He flies in this region of fire, without burning himself; he walks above the stars, like on stones in a river, without shipwreck. He pours out, with true love, into the bosom of his spiritual brothers and all the choirs of angels. And as from time to time he fixes the gaze of his thoughts on the course of the sun, and on the phases of the moon and the theory of the stars, he does so through his brothers (*the angels*), lest he envy them, and lest he weaken them in bodily occupation; his Lord gives him from time to time power over these stars, so that they move according to his command, as we see with Joshua, son of Nun, who stopped one at Gibeon, and the other in the valley of Ayalon'. Isaiah in turn ordered it

REASON FOR THE FOUNDING OF THE SCHOOL

to move back ten degrees, and thus he taught his peers that the stars are creatures and not creators.

In short, to sum up, God gave man, for his instruction, power over everything that exists, above as well as below, over the sea and the land, over fish and reptiles, over quadrupeds and every animal, over birds and every swift bird. He uses it, at will, either for his nourishment, or for his use, or for his pleasure, as well as for his clothing.

But intelligence, having acted against the first instruction it had received, having blinded the eye of its discernment without understanding the reason, and having listened to the words of the deceiver, his old brother, who sinned first and fell from his dignity, the one who is a liar and the father of lies, he who always takes care of the sons of disobedience, consequently this sentence (apóphasis) was passed against him: You are dust and you will return. to dust, and you will eat the grass of the fields.' However, he did not deprive him of instruction and teaching. But, through many vicissitudes, he made himself known to him, lest once abandoned, he perished completely and became a vessel of perdition.

But it is to the older spiritual powers in the order of creation and more noble by nature that he shared his knowledge, so that they would not fall into error and not think of themselves as great. He wrote to the angels with the finger of his creative power a scroll of intangible light, and aloud he read it before them saying: Let there be light, and there was light. And as they were endowed with an intelligent mentality, they immediately understood that everything that is done is done by another, and that the one to whom an order is given, receives it from the One who has the command. And from there they knew for certain that the one who gave being to this excellent nature, is the one who created them too. Therefore, all of them, with one unanimous and loud voice, gave thanks to their Creator, as it is written in Job: When I created the morning stars, all my angels sang with a loud voice and glorified me.

And just as we have a habit, which consists of this: after reading simple letters in front of the child and having them repeat them, we join them together and build names out of them so that they can spell them and practice, so did this eternal Master. After repeating the alphabet to the angels, he formed a great name out of it, that of the completion of the firmament, and he read it to them so that they would understand that he is the Creator of all, and that everything fulfills his will, as he commands. Now, the angels, being of a penetrating spirit and quickly absorbing the teachings, God taught them all the certain science in six days, sometimes through the gathering of waters and the production of trees, sometimes through the formation of reptiles and the creation of animals, sometimes through the division of stars and the creation of birds, until he had placed the number ten in their hands. Finally, in forming man, he gave them the final lesson. Then he handed over to them the visible creatures, as if they were letters to write, based on their continuous evolutions, and to spell out the name of the Creator and the Organizer of all things. He left them in regions where they can enjoy much more than in this spacious house of the school of the earth. He provided them, to enjoy endlessly and not be idle, in this house of darkness, earthly house; and he never ceases to take care of the disobedient children.

As for Gabriel and Michael with their companions, because they applied themselves to their lesson and did not tire of the beatific meditation, he made them his familiars and the guests of his palace. They always stand in his presence and rejoice in the manifestations (of his glory), as Daniel said, "Thousands upon thousands stood before him, and ten thousand times ten thousand attended him." He distributed them into nine choirs (ráqua) and gave them nine functions. And although they all have one nature, nevertheless he made them Seraphim, which means sanctifiers, Watchers, who constantly watch before his Majesty; others, he made them Cherubim, who carry and exalt the throne of God, bound by straps of fire, and from which occasionally bursts forth a dazzling light upon all; others, he made them princes of the peoples; others, rulers of the kingdoms; to others he gave the title of Powers, to be able to carry out his orders; others, he named Angels, which means "the sent ones"; others, he honored with the name of Thrones, a name that shows the greatness of their glory. And these, as it seems, are higher than all; finally, to others he applies the name of archangels (apxós) which expresses their authority over all. In short, there is no one among them to whom he has not given some degree of glory, according to the merit of his knowledge. This is how God directed this spiritual school.

REASON FOR THE FOUNDING OF THE SCHOOL

Let us now come to ours, and see how he governed it, and in what manner he conducted himself towards it, and with what letters he constructed names, so that he could read them and practice.

As soon as he created Adam and Eve, he made all the animals and beasts pass before them, in order of letters. He inspired him invisibly so that he could read them aloud. Adam read in these first tablets names for all the animals, for all the beasts of the desert and the birds of the sky; and the name that Adam gave to every living animal, became its name. After Adam had repeated these unwritten letters well, forming exact names, God transported his school to the garden of Eden; and there, he taught them the commandments and laws. First, he wrote a small psalm for them about the tree that was beautiful to look at, for them to read and learn the difference between good and evil. And as God knew their weakness, he threatened them with these terms: The day you erase one of the letters on these tablets, and when you eat from the fruit of this tree, your instructor, you will die.' However, not only did he not leave him in this threat, but he promised him, as a master to his student, and as a father to his children, that if he read and meditated on this commandment, and if, at the appointed time, he repeated the names he had read before him, and showed all the letters without erasing them, he would give him the tree of life, to eat from and live eternally.

But his older brother, seeing his glory and the tablets that were written for him, thinking that if he read them, as he had been ordered, and repeated the names marked on them, not only would he preserve the name of the image and likeness (of God), but he would also receive the perfection of nature, like the deceiver, and that the sting of death would no longer pierce him, he went away and wrote other tablets contrary to the first ones. He accused God before them, saying: "You will die," you have been told; this is not true. If you eat from this tree by disobeying the command of your Lord, you will be like gods, knowing good and evil[2]. With these words, this tree pleased their eyes, like the pumpkin to Jonah. At that moment both together broke the yoke, broke the bonds, threw the tablets on the ground, and erased the letters of the commandment. Then the wise Master came, and seeing the tablets thrown on the ground, letters erased, and (Adam and Eve) stripped and naked, immediately he punished them like children; he made them leave that school and sent them to the earth, from where

REASON FOR THE FOUNDING OF THE SCHOOL

they were formed, to work and eat until they returned to the earth, from where they had been taken.

He then established a third school, that of Abel and Cain; he demanded from them, as the price of his teaching, sacrifices and offerings. But as Cain became like the deceiver, his companion, and envied the honor of his brother, to whom he dealt a deadly blow, just as Satan had killed Adam, as Our Lord said: From the beginning he is a murderer and does not remain in the truth, he also delivered him to the terrible punishments of fear and dread; he drove him from his presence and said to him: When you till the ground, it shall no longer yield to you its strength. You shall be a fugitive and a wanderer on the earth. Then Cain went away from the presence of the Lord and settled in the land of Nod, east of Eden.

He then established for Noah a school full of beautiful meanings, bearing the mark of mercy. This school lasted for a hundred years: for every day he explained to him the meaning of the glorious economy (providence). And because he worked beyond his strength, and received the teaching of the fear of God with diligence and understanding, God saved him from the punishment of the flood; He preserved him to be a shoot in the world, and to renew the effigy (of God) that had been erased. He brought him out of that cursed school by the ship that carried the world. He brought him into this spacious region, full of all the beauties of virtue; He testified that Noah was righteous and full of integrity in his time. As a reward for his righteousness, He promised him that He would no longer curse the earth because of man; but as long as the earth endures, seedtime and harvest, summer and winter, day and night shall not cease.

He then established another school, in the time of the blessed Abraham; He brought him out of his homeland and family, and brought him to the plain of Haran. There, He taught him what was necessary. Then He brought him to the land of Palestine. And as He tested him for a long time and found him worthy. From his school, he agreed to enter his home and dine with him. And because of his virtues, he promised him that he would multiply his descendants like the sand on the seashore, and like the stars in the sky: I know Abraham, said the Lord, and I know that he will command his children and his household after him to keep the way of the Lord, to do what is right and just. He also gave him immense wealth and crowned him with a great old age. He

REASON FOR THE FOUNDING OF THE SCHOOL

established a great school of perfect philosophy in the time of Moses. Having brought the Israelites out of Egypt, he led them to Mount Sinai, where, having appointed Moses as his administrator, he poured out his glory and splendor upon him. His love even made him come down to them with troops of angels, to visit them and to recite to them again orders and laws. And since it was very difficult for them to receive lessons from this eternal mouth, Moses, the school principal, upon their request, received the order to transmit to them the life-giving voice of God: Speak with us yourself, they said to him, and we will listen, but let not God speak with us, lest we die. Therefore, Moses spoke with God and God made his voice heard to him. But God, knowing the coarseness of their thoughts and the hardness of their spirit would also drive them, like their brothers, to transgress his laws and trample upon his doctrine, wrote the Ten Commandments, which he gave them on stone tablets so that they would never be erased.

And when Moses and his lieutenant descended from the mountain, having heard noise in the school, Joshua said to Moses: What is this noise of battle in the camp? And Moses replied: It is not the sound of victors, nor the sound of the vanquished, but I hear the sound of sin. So Moses became angry and broke the two tablets. Upon his arrival at the school, having seen a new teacher unconscious, seated on the chair, and the people amusing themselves as they pleased in front of him, accepting the false as true and taking away from Moses his role as administrator and from Joshua all the respect due to him, Moses, I say, then became angry, subjected the new teacher to the terrible punishment of the whip, threw him off his throne, reduced him to dust with a file, scattered his powder in the waters, made the confused disciples drink it, and resounded his voice in the school saying: Let he who is for the Lord come to me. Immediately all the notable brothers, children of Levi, gathered around him. It seems that these were not inclined towards the error. Moses ordered them to each take their sword, to go back and forth from door to door through the camp, and not to spare even their brothers and children. They carried out his order. Then he said to them: "You have sanctified your hands to the Lord." And so they caused to perish all those on whom could be seen, after drinking the aforesaid water, any sign of their love for the calf.

Then Moses, having calmed down, turned to the Lord and prayed for reconciliation with his disciples and not to remember their fault, on the pretext that they were still children. The Lord granted Moses'

REASON FOR THE FOUNDING OF THE SCHOOL

prayer and ordered him to make tablets like the first ones, to write on them the ten commandments and to come down from the mountain to read them to the people. Out of respect for Moses, and to show that his prayer had been answered, the Lord made his face shine with light and glory, and not wanting to instruct the enraged people himself, he entrusted them with the school and appointed him as a teacher in his place. Moses descended from the mountain and read the ten commandments to the Israelites, who were willing to repeat them and observe all that was ordered. Then this first teacher among mortals also wrote new commandments for them, which were more numerous and more difficult (to observe) than the first ones, as he himself said: "I imposed severe decrees and laws on them, so that they do not live by them, and the man who follows them will live by them.'

He led this school for forty years in the desert of Horeb. Whoever needed to consult the Lord would go to Moses; he would sit diligently from morning to evening, resolving all questions and difficulties. As for those who opposed his teachings, as punishment for their crimes, he would either strike them with a terrible blow of the sword, or swallow them up by the earth, or devour them by fire, or finally he would excommunicate them, as it happened to Aaron and Mary, who was locked outside the camp for seven days and had to confess her fault. As a reward for his precision in leading this school, God ordered that he not be buried by the Israelites, but by God himself and his angels in the mountain.

At his death, he entrusted the school to his lieutenant Joshua, as inspired by the Lord, so that he would be his successor in leading the school and teach there with precision. Joshua introduced the Israelites to the promised land, subjugated the lost peoples and made the division of the promised land as it should be. After his death, there was no king in Israel; as the Scripture says, but everyone did what seemed right to them, until the time when the prophet Samuel and King David were elected and instructed the people of God.

Solomon also founded a school; he instructed both his subjects and foreigners: All the kings of the earth, it is said, came to hear the Wisdom of Solomon. Solomon, in fact, having been proclaimed king, asked only for wisdom, which would enable him to judge and lead his people fairly; so God granted him extraordinary wisdom. "Behold," He said to him, "I have given you a wise and discerning heart, so that there

REASON FOR THE FOUNDING OF THE SCHOOL

has been no one like you before you, nor shall anyone arise like you after you." And the Scripture testifies about him and says: "He was wiser than any other man; he spoke about the virtues and influences of all bodies, from the cedar in Lebanon to the hyssop that grows out of the wall; and he also spoke about the animals of the earth, the birds, the reptiles, and the fish." He sometimes calls his disciples sons. "Listen, my son," he said, "and receive my words and the years of your life will be multiplied.' To everything, he said again, there is a season, and to every matter under the heavens, there is a time.

He also sometimes gives his students lessons about God: "When you enter the house of God," he said, "be careful with your steps, and approach to listen rather than to offer the sacrifice of fools[3]. And since there were many scholars at that time who thought they had understood God and even His power, wisdom, and operations, Solomon alone said that it is impossible for the intelligence of creatures and fleshly beings to understand God: "I said," he wrote, "I will acquire wisdom; but it has distanced itself from me more than distance itself. Who can find the depth of depths', that is, who can understand the divine essence? Who is the man who could come to judgment after the king, and then with the one who created him? The sky is high, the earth is deep, there is no way to fathom the heart of the divine king.

In short, in his old age, he gathered all the people near him and spoke to them about the weakness of this world, demonstrating that it is transient and fleeting with its pleasures and everything is vanity. And when he advises what is best, he says: Fear God and keep his commandments; for God will bring to judgment everything that has been done, with everything hidden, whether good or bad."

The other prophets also founded schools, as we learn from the history of the blessed prophet Elisha. According to the tradition of his master Elijah, he followed the path of his predecessors and taught for a long time what was necessary in the school he had founded.

The Scripture clearly states: The sons of the prophets said to Elisha: The place where we are sitting before you is too small for us. Let us go to the Jordan and each of us take a piece of wood from there, and we will build a place to live, and you will come with us too. And he replied: Go and do it, and I will come with you. The holy Scripture shows by

REASON FOR THE FOUNDING OF THE SCHOOL

these words that it was a school that the sons of the prophets founded in the desert; and it was to gather and escape the noise of the world, and thus be able to more easily receive the lessons of their master, that they went out into the desert.

To avoid being too verbose in our speech, we will pass over in silence. All the other assemblies that the other prophets formed, to arrive at the assemblies that the pagan philosophers gathered. They tried to imitate the Jewish assemblies; but, as the foundation of their instruction was not based on the truth of faith, and they did not take as their starting point the principle of wisdom, which is the fear of the Lord, they completely strayed from the truth. For, having compared everything according to the order of nature, they could not understand anything; and calling themselves wise, they became foolish because they worshiped and served the creatures more than the Creator. The first one who formed assemblies in Athens was Plato; it is reported of him that he had more than a thousand students. Aristotle himself was in his school. One day, while giving lessons to his disciples, noticing that Aristotle was absent, he said: "The friend of wisdom is absent; where is the seeker of the beautiful? I have a thousand, and one is missing; one, for me, is worth more than a thousand."

Plato, although he spoke rightly of God, and said of His only Son that, as Word, He is begotten of Him, that is, of His substance, and that the Holy Spirit is the personal virtue that proceeds from Him, nevertheless, having been questioned by his fellow citizens, whether or not to respect the idols, Plato, I say, answered them affirmatively: "One must," he said, "sacrifice a white rooster to Asclepius." Having known God, he did not glorify Him as God and did not give thanks to Him; but he wandered in vain reasonings, and his heart, lacking understanding, was filled with darkness and did not comprehend. (He taught metempsychosis): the soul, he said, dwells sometimes in reptiles, in animals, sometimes in birds, then in man, then, after taking the form of angels and enrolling in their hierarchy, it purifies itself and returns to its celestial abode. He also taught, like the Manichaeans, the community of women. After his death, he was succeeded by Aristotle; the latter contradicted the teaching and tradition of his master, to assert his own. Among other absurdities that he rambled on, he taught that the economy and providence of God only govern creatures up to the moon. As for other creatures, he entrusted their governance to the Principalities.

REASON FOR THE FOUNDING OF THE SCHOOL

There were also assemblies in Babylon of the Chaldeans, where for a long time seven (planets) and twelve constellations (zodiac signs) have been taught. There were also schools in India and Egypt, the errors of which would be difficult for us to explain.

Epicurus and Democritus formed assemblies in Alexandria; they taught that this world is eternal and exists by itself: "There were first, they said, fine bodies, which, because of their extreme fineness, escape the senses; and they designate them as immaterial atoms. However, they add, these atoms have neither soul, nor reason, nor beginning, nor generation, nor end, so numerous they are."

There was also an assembly of those designated as Physicists, who claimed, among other things, that inorganic elements were the principles of the universe; they therefore denied the existence of God and Providence, saying that the strong plunder and the weak are plundered. Pythagoras, although he taught the unity of God, creation, and Providence, nevertheless mixed many errors with these truths.

Zoroaster, a Persian mage, also founded a school in Persia, at the time. From the king Baschtasp, he attracted many students, who, being blind in mind, easily agreed with him in his errors. He first taught the existence of four gods: Aschoukar, Praschoukar, Zaroukar' and Zarwan; but he did not say what their operations were. Then he admitted two other gods Hormezd and Ahriman, saying that both were born of Zarwan: Hormezd is completely good; Ahriman is completely bad. These are the two who created this world: the good god created the good creatures, and the evil god created the bad creatures. Zoroaster then admitted twenty-four other gods, making a total of thirty according to the days of the months. He said that animals should not be slaughtered; because Hormezd is in them, but that the animal intended to be slaughtered should be beaten with a stick on the neck until it was lifeless, and then sacrificed so that it did not feel the pain. He also said, among other things, that a man can marry his mother, his daughter and her sister; and that the dead should not be buried, but thrown outside to be food for birds of prey. These were the assemblies founded by the sons of error. Although they founded them for their own good and for the good of others, the results show that they only taught error, lost souls, and obscured minds. Together they broke the yoke and bonds of the Lord our God: Truth, says David, has perished

REASON FOR THE FOUNDING OF THE SCHOOL

from the earth. Lord, says Jeremiah, may your eyes be attentive to preserve the faith, that is, the truth of your essence. All these assemblies, claiming to be wise, have become foolish. And elsewhere it says: They were ashamed of what they trusted in. So it was necessary for the Bright Wisdom, the Master of masters, the eternal Ray, the living Word of God, to come to the earth. He renewed the first school of his father, altered by the sons of error. He invited them to come to Him: Come to me, He cried, all you who labor and are burdened, and I will give you rest. And first of all, He appointed John the Baptist, master of reading and preacher, and the apostle Peter, the steward of the school, said: "all the prophets and the law have prophesied until John, and since then the kingdom of heaven is announced, and he urges everyone to enter it. John gives all his attention to the school; he rebukes, teaches, and blames the wicked and the lazy in the desert, on the banks of the Jordan. He is also tasked with administering the baptism of repentance for the remission of sins; and Our Lord testifies that among those born of women, none greater than him has been raised up. As soon as John manifested and showed to all this source of wisdom and the true Master, saying: Behold the one who bears the sin of the world, then all the people began to gather around him and listen to his teaching.

The glory of Our Lord increased day by day, the assembly of John began to decrease, as well as his glory, as John himself said: He must increase, but I must decrease. As soon as Our Lord took the lead of this school, and a numerous crowd came to him, He chose distinguished brothers, namely Peter, John, and their companions. He made them go up a high mountain, thus His Father made on Mount Sinai, and there He initiated them into the knowledge of His Father and His knowledge, He trained them in the manner and purpose of His teaching; He explained to them all the difficulties of the law, and He clarified before them all the allegories and shadows of the Old Testament, just as He Himself said, "I have come not to abolish the law, but to fulfill it." Just as painters do not begin by applying bright colors to the image, suitable to the reality of the type, but draw it with charcoal, or trace simple lines, and only after the model is perfected and takes the complete form of a real image, do they adorn it with splendid hues of dazzling colors, similar to those of the type, so does the great master of the universe act.

REASON FOR THE FOUNDING OF THE SCHOOL

And what do I say? Behold, even the artists, when they want to cast a statue, first begin by painting all the features of it on the ground; and after thus representing the statue in wax and comparing all the features together, they cast gold or copper onto the wax, and as soon as the wax is consumed, they have a complete and enduring image in copper. Now, wise men not only do not consider the loss of the first image as damage, but they see in it the skill of the artist, who by the loss of the aforementioned matter, could form a real image that will always remain.

This was how the great Master first acted according to the childhood of the students. As the figure of the real knowledge of God was about to melt and consume, He sent His beloved Son. who, basing His instruction on the first figure, spoke to us and revealed to us the real image of the Holy Trinity, future life, the abrogation of the old law and the consummation of its weak precepts, and engraved in our minds the reality of truth: "When He went up the mountain, it is said, and a great crowd gathered around Him, opening His mouth. He taught them, saying: Blessed are the poor in spirit, for theirs is the kingdom of heaven, etc. Elsewhere it is written that having gone up into a boat, He taught many things to the crowd through parables. At other times, He taught in the temple and in the synagogues, as He himself said to the Jews: I was with you every day, teaching in the temple, and you did not seize me. The number of His disciples was so considerable that the chief priests and the Pharisees were struck with jealousy. As they themselves testified by saying: You see that everyone is going after him, if we leave him like this, everyone will believe in Him'. So just as the wax image achieves its fulfillment and not its annihilation in the copper image, because even though the wax melts, its figure remains enduring, so also Christ did not abolish the law and its figures, but He completed and fulfilled them, as He himself said.

At the age of thirty, he began to give lessons, renewed the first school, gave a precise definition of philosophy, resurrected the dead wisdom, revived the fear of God that had disappeared, showed the truth that was lost; in short, He shaped all kinds of sciences like the limbs of a statue, distinct from each other, and engraved them in the ears of the faithful; he rebuked impiety, made error disappear, and confounded imposture. After writing his testament to them in the cenacle, at the time of his passion, he led his disciples, and went with them beyond the brook Kidron, and there he gave them lessons all night long on the

REASON FOR THE FOUNDING OF THE SCHOOL

great, admirable, and real mysteries. And since their senses were still too weak to embrace such a perfect doctrine, He said to them: I would still have many things to tell you, but they are still beyond your understanding. When the Spirit of truth comes, He will teach you all the truth.

After He was resurrected on the third day, as He had said, He stayed with them in the world for forty days, teaching them many things. At the moment of His Ascension to heaven, He chose twelve renowned brothers; He recommended to them what was necessary and essential. Go, He said to them, and instruct all nations, baptizing them in the name of the Father, and of the Son, and of the Holy Spirit, and teaching them to observe all that I have commanded you. And behold, I am always with you until the end of the world.

As their leader, He gave them Simon the steward of the school and commanded him to shepherd men, women, and children. After He ascended to heaven, the Apostles did what their Master had commanded them, preaching everywhere, as Mark said. Our Lord worked with them and confirmed their word with the miracles they performed. They first established their school in the cenacle, where Our Lord had given them the holy sacrament, and kept it there until the Holy Spirit descended. They then came to Antioch, where they taught and baptized many people, so that it was in Antioch, as Luke says, that the disciples began to be called Christians. Soon after, Our Lord chose the great Paul to teach all the Gentiles. This fervent disciple and diligent teacher, who surpasses both the first and the last, gathered brothers in several places and founded schools in Damascus, Arabia, Achaia, and Corinth, where he taught for two and a half years. Then, after fourteen years of work, he went to Jerusalem intending to see the Apostles, but he soon returned to continue his work. He had to endure many hardships and sufferings. Is someone afflicted? He said, that I am not also afflicted? Is someone scandalized? that I am not also consumed? He did not cease to engage with all the heretics and opposing opinions until he had shaped them to the manner of his doctrine. Coming from Corinth to Ephesus, he met twelve disciples there and spoke boldly to them for three months, as recognized by Luke in the Acts of the Apostles, to convince them of the truths concerning the kingdom of God. Some were insulting his doctrine, he withdrew and separated the disciples from them, teaching every day in the school of a man named Tyrannus; and this continued for two years,

REASON FOR THE FOUNDING OF THE SCHOOL

so that all those who lived in Asia heard the word of God. Up to this point, we have not even had the name of the school, which means a place of intellectual instruction.

After Saint Paul had completed the course of his instruction in all corners of the earth, and had received, in Rome, with Saint Peter, the crown of martyrdom under the impious Nero, and after all the Apostles had been taken to be with Our Lord, the wicked foxes then began to stick their heads out of their dens, to enter the delightful vineyard, ruin it, and also demolish the first tradition that Our Lord had passed on to his Apostles. The party of Satan thus began to grow strong, while the school of the good Master began to weaken. The great Master, seeing the weakness of his party and the strength of the opposing party, chose and appointed intelligent teachers in his school to lead according to his will.

Now that, with the help of God, we have arrived here, we must first demonstrate where schools began to be opened after the death of the glorious Apostles, and at what time and by whom the Scriptures began to be explained. The subject of our dissertation will naturally lead us to talk about this school where we study. The school of Alexandria was very famous, as we have said; its reputation and antiquity attracted many people to receive lessons in philosophy. And, as the taste for study is innate in the human race, there was a zeal for learning, who, educated in Christian sciences, founded a school of Holy Scripture in the aforementioned city, so that it would not be thought that sciences are only found among pagans. In addition to the reading of these holy books, he also added, as an adornment, commentary which sometimes led him to distort the truth contained in the Scripture with very bizarre imaginations. The director of this school was the Jew Philo, who, as soon as he embraced this art, began to explain the Scripture through allegories, to the detriment of history. These wise men did not understand that they should not only avoid teaching. They aimed at trifles, but also adorned the divine Books with a true doctrine; they therefore loved human glory more than divine glory. Now those who frequented Alexandria, for the purpose of instruction, were very numerous. Soon the school of philosophers disappeared, and the new school became prosperous. After the death of Philo, the wicked Arius became famous in Alexandria; he promised a thorough discussion concerning the divine books; he had even acquired secular erudition. Having been called upon to explain the Scriptures, he, in the intoxication of pride, invented a new and false doctrine, saying that the Son is created.

A council was summoned against him at Nicaea, under Eustathius, bishop of Antioch, an ecumenical council, which lasted three years and anathematized the doctrine of Arius. The council also dealt with all the heresies that had appeared in the Church from the time of the Apostles until then. The discussion against all the heresies lasted forty days, the response of the Fathers to their objections fifteen days, and the drafting of the canons and their causes three days.

After the conclusion of the council, the blessed Eustathius opened a school in his city of Antioch, and James in Nisibis - - for this saint also attended the council, and Alexander in Alexandria. We do not intend to speak of all these schools. Mar Ephrem was appointed as a commentator by James, and Athanasius by Alexander. As for Eustathius, having been exiled, he entrusted the leadership of the assembly to Saint Flavian, who, for such a matter, was associated with Diodore. They guided the assembly of Antioch on the path of orthodoxy, disregarding the threats of King Valens and the insolence of the Arians, sons of error, but carrying out their works sometimes within the city and sometimes outside.

When Flavian was consecrated bishop, the blessed Diodorus retired to a convent, where he opened a school that he directed for a long time; he had many disciples, among whom were the blessed Basil, John (Chrysostom), Evagrius and Theodore the Great (of Mopsuestia), who drew from him the science of the Scriptures. Diodore, indeed, was more accomplished than any other in the science of philosophy and in exegesis.

This saint, having been consecrated bishop of Tarsus, his disciples dispersed, and only the blessed Theodore remained in the monastery, who alone taught there for a long time, not only orally, but also by composing works, at the request of the Fathers. By the power of grace, he made commentaries on all the Books and controversies against all heresies. Until the time when grace revealed this man on earth, all branches of instruction, exegesis, and traditions on the divine Scriptures, like the different materials used to make the image of the King of kings, were scattered and dispersed everywhere without order in the works of the early writers and the Fathers of the Catholic Church.

As soon as this man distinguished between good and evil, and learned from the writings and traditions of the early (writers), then, like a skillful physician, he united all the traditions and chapters into one body, which were scattered, so that he adapted them to each other with the beauty of art and intelligence; he prepared and combined perfect and very beautiful instructive remedies, which uproot and make disappear from the minds of those who take them with desire, all the troublesome diseases of ignorance. Certainly, our body is subject to many diseases and sufferings, but the disease of not knowing is the most terrible and the most harmful to our souls. Just as those who want to make a statue, first begin to shape each member separately, and then adapt them one by one, as required by the laws of art, and perfect the statue, so did the blessed Theodore, having arranged, coordinated, adjusted, and cast each of the members of this science into a divine mold, fashioned in all his books a perfect and admirable image of the infinitely blessed divine essence. And in him was fulfilled what was said of Solomon: He was wiser than all those who were before and after him. Such was the work of Theodore for fifty years. During his episcopal life in Mopsuestia, he always went to pray at the tomb of the blessed Thecla, and asked her for help in order to be able to explain the Scriptures.

At his death, as the blessed Nestorius had already been elected patriarch of Constantinople, he charged his disciple Theodulus to teach in his place in Mopsuestia. Theodulus lived until the time of the blessed Mar Narsai and Barsauma, bishops, who went to see him to receive his blessing: witness Akhsenaias, a wicked worker, who said that in his time he was still alive.

[Despite the esteem that the world had for Theodore, Rabbulas, bishop of Edessa, despised him greatly]. Rabbulas had previously shown much friendship to the famous Interpreter and studied his works. But, having gone to Constantinople to attend the council of the Fathers, he was accused of striking the clergy; having replied that Our Lord also struck, when he entered the temple, the Interpreter stood up and rebuked him, saying: "Our Lord did not do that; to men, he only spoke, saying, 'Take this away from here,' and overturned the tables. But he drove out with a whip the bulls and sheep." Rabbulas, from then on, held a grudge against him in his heart; and after his death, he had all his writings burned in Edessa. Only the commentaries on John the Evangelist and on Ecclesiastes escaped the fire, as they were reportedly not yet translated from Greek to Syriac. But what we have said about Theodore is enough.

Let us now show how, for what reason, and by whom this divine assembly was transferred to Persia. The blessed Mar Ephrem, whom we mentioned earlier, when the city of Nisibis was handed over to the Persians, withdrew to Edessa, where he spent the rest of his life; he opened a school there and had many disciples. After his death, the school, far from declining, made considerable progress, thanks to the activity of his disciples, who increased the assembly. The school's reputation spread everywhere, and many young people, out of love for wisdom, came from all parts to attend. When Mar Narsai, Barsauma, and Ma'né, who were later consecrated bishops of Nisibis and the latter Rewardaschir heard the fame of this school, as they were studious men, they went there immediately with the others.

The director and interpreter of the school at that time was Cyoré; he had a very enlightened spirit; he was all for God; he was so consumed by the love of teaching that he took it upon himself to interpret, teach reading, spell, and preach in the church. Despite his youth and mortifications, he carefully fulfilled all these duties. The only thing he regretted was that the Interpreter's commentaries had not yet been translated into Syriac. For commentary, he used the traditions written by Saint Ephrem, and emanated, according to what is said, from the mouth of the Apostle Addai, who, as the first, was the founder of this assembly of Edessa; because he and his student had gone to Edessa and had sown this precious seed there. And even what we call the Tradition of the school does not mean the Interpreter's commentaries, but those that have been preserved from the beginning. From mouth to ear, and which the blessed Narsai inserted in his homilies and in the rest of his works.
The comments of Theodore having been translated into Syriac and having passed to the assembly of Edessa, Cyorus enjoyed rest with all his disciples.

The saints, whom we mentioned earlier, remained for a long time at the feet of this blessed one; they were versed in the interpretation of divine books and in their tradition, and they studied the writings of the Interpreter.

After the death of Cyorus, the interpreter of the school, the whole assembly asked for Narsai to be their leader and director; for he had no equal in the school. Narsai, unable to resist, said to them: "I cannot take on all the work of the school, like our master, who was experienced and rich in health of body and grace of spirit. But if you establish a reading master and another for spelling, I may be able to take on the interpretation." The assembly granted his request. Narsai led the school for twenty years, making daily commentaries accompanied by singing.

Barsauma came to Nisibis and was elected bishop. Ma'né left for Persia and received the yoke of priesthood there. The affairs of the school were in good order, but Satan, as was his custom, sowed discord and disorder. Mar Narsai then left the school and, having come to Nisibis, settled in the convent of the Persians. He had planned to go to Persia. Barsauma, upon learning this, sent his archdeacon to him and had him brought into the city with great honor. After greeting each other and spending a few days together, Barsauma asked Narsai to stay with him and establish a school in the city, promising his support. Narsai, hesitating to accept his request, said, "Do not think, my brother, that your departure from Edessa and the scattering of the assembly are accidental; on the contrary, they are providential. You would not be wrong, if you compare this incident to the one that took place in Jerusalem, after the Ascension of Our Lord. There, too, were the assembly of the Apostles, the gifts of the Holy Spirit, miracles, and all kinds of virtues. As the inhabitants of that city did not deserve it, their home was deserted, as our Redeemer said. But the Apostles, going along the paths that lead to the cities of the Gentiles and into the enclosures of the pagans, gathered all those they found, bad or good; they preached, baptized, and instructed; and thus, in a short time, the Gospel of Our Lord spread throughout the world. Now, in my opinion, the dispersion of this assembly is quite similar to that of the Apostles. If you listen to me, and settle here, you will do much good everywhere. You cannot find a more suitable city for you in all of Persia than this one; it is an important city; and, as it is located between the two empires, people come from all sides; when they learn that there is a school here and especially that you are its director, they will flock to you. You will be an intrepid soldier, and you will serve as a shield for us in times when heresy began to target Mesopotamia openly. Perhaps

REASON FOR THE FOUNDING OF THE SCHOOL

you and I can eliminate this evil from the land. Two are better than one; for they have a good reward for their labor; and if one is stronger, two will withstand him.'"

Barsauma was able, by these words and others like them, to calm the spirit of Narsai, who was willing to establish a school in Nisibis. He immediately ordered everything necessary for a school to be prepared. In a short time, he attracted many brothers, so that not only Persian and Syrian brothers came to him, but also most of the brothers who were in the school of Edessa. Everyone glorified God. Schools multiplied in the Persian empire; Edessa darkened; Nisibis shone; the Roman Empire was filled with error, while the Persian Empire was filled with the knowledge of the fear of God. Narsai led this school for forty-five years; he also composed more than three hundred homilies along with other works.

Barsauma also composed many homilies with other instructions. Both lived according to the divine will and were transported to their Master. It is not the story of their virtues that we set out to tell, but the manner of their teaching. After the death of Narsai, Mar Elisha Bar Qosbaye served as the interpreter for seven years; he was a great and learned man in all ecclesiastical and profane books. He also composed many works, treatises refuting the doctrines of the Magi, controversies against heretics, and commentaries on all the books of the Old Testament, in the Syriac language. After Elisha had peacefully passed away in extreme old age, Mar Abraham succeeded him. He was related to Mar Narsai; he even served him and lived in the same cell with him. His name was. It is said, Narsai; but as soon as he was brought by his father to this blessed man, he changed his name and called him Abraham, so that he would not be called by his master's name. It is even said that John of Beth Rabban was also called Abraham. When he came to them, they named him John, so that he would not be called by his fellow disciple's name. Abraham and John, having drunk from the source of wisdom, were able to lead the assembly with all the fear of God. John worked hard in the School; and, if we must tell the truth, all the good orders found there come from this saint. He also composed commentaries and traditions on the Scriptures, treatises of controversy against the Jews and against Eutyches. He also wrote three speeches, one when Chosroes seized Nigran, because he was there at the Gate for School affairs; the other two are on the Rogations and on the plague; he has other works as well.

John was carried away by the great plague. Then the burden of Abraham doubled in weight: he led the assembly for sixty years, diligently applying himself to the young, to prayer, supporting long vigils, working day and night, interpreting (Scripture), singing songs, and providing solutions to questions. He also composed commentaries on the prophets, on Ecclesiastes, on Joshua, and on the Judges. It is not necessary for me to speak of the great works he did in the school, the magnificent buildings he erected there, and the considerable profits he made for it because his works are more evident and more notorious than the rays of the sun; all of Persia was illuminated by his instruction; he too was, like the patriarch Abraham, the father of many populations; he begot countless spiritual children, and he inherited a good reputation, in the kingdom of the Persians as well as in that of the Romans.

When this holy and blessed father was also gathered up, into the storeroom of celestial life, like sheaves piled up in their time, Mar Jésu'yahb.

Arzounaia succeeded him in the direction of the school; he worked there with admirable strength; but, after two years, feeling tired, he left and became the bishop of Arzoun; he was later elected patriarch. The chair of interpretation was passed on to Mar Abraham of Nisibus, a tall man, knowledgeable in all sciences, zealous, courageous, master in the fear of God, hardworking and diligent. After trading for a year with this spiritual talent, he also fell asleep with his spiritual fathers. He was replaced by Nana of Adiabene, a man adorned with humility, and with all the gifts of instruction required for the work of interpretation; and if someone says that is why he was elected from the beginning, they will not be wrong; moreover, the sequence of events clearly demonstrates this. He indeed went through many trials; having emptied his quiver against the devil's party, the devil unleashed terrible agitations against him, violent troubles, and unspeakable disputes, quarrels, and schisms. But Divine providence did not allow any of the fiery darts of the evil one to pierce him. Having set foot on the rock of faith and lowered his shoulder to better engage in spiritual work, he never ceased to fight, according to the divine will, in the spiritual arena (radov); he applied himself day and night to reading and interpreting the Scriptures, like the blessed Paul, he invited and urged everyone to this work. Considering his ardent love for interpretation, the firmness of his speech, and the immense richness of his soul, not only did he not content himself with giving us interpretation through speech, but he also wanted to preserve for us in writing, like the blessed Interpreter, his views and opinions on all the verses and chapters of the Old and New Testaments. He also composed many homilies and hymns.

We all pray to God to prolong his days, as he prolonged the life of Hezekiah; because his soul, like the great treasure of the State, is rich in all the knowledge of the Scriptures. Just as the king's table is adorned with all kinds of food, so too he always serves us a spiritual table, laden with excellent dishes drawn from the Books, embellished with all kinds of teachings from holy reading and elevated by the beautiful words of the philosophers. Whoever is nourished by him no longer needs any other food. For, just as every well-instructed doctor in matters concerning the kingdom of heaven brings out, as it is said, from his treasure new and old things and feeds hungry souls, so too he nourishes us through his works sometimes with old things, sometimes with new things, and sometimes with the writings of the ancients.

He is sweet, merciful, patient, and does not seek his own glory like others. His writings are spread everywhere; he is present and teaches through his writings even where he is not. Thanks to his disciples, his fame and reputation have filled all nearby schools as well as those that are distant. That is why we pray and beseech God, the universal Providence, that when he decides to take him with him, to choose us. At least among his children and disciples, someone who is like him in manners and customs, who follows his traditions and always respects his memory, as a child respects that of his father.

This is, in short, the reason for the Assemblies. It is not without reason that the session was established and set during the two seasons of summer and winter. Man is composed of body and soul, which cannot exist without each other. The Fathers, seeing us caring for our spiritual nourishment, also set a time for us to work to feed our bodies. Our Lord Himself, when teaching the apostles the purpose of spiritual prayer, showed them that food for the body is also necessary: Give us this day our daily bread, he made them say. Paul also teaches the same thing: We brought nothing into the world, and it is evident that we can take nothing out of it; but as long as we have food and clothing, that will be enough for us. The Fathers also acted in the same way, fixing

REASON FOR THE FOUNDING OF THE SCHOOL

the two works to the two seasons before the summer session, first comes the harvest. And then the session of the Apostles'; and before the winter session comes the work of figs and olives and then the winter session. Our Fathers taught us to apply ourselves zealously to these two works; but let us know which of these two works is meant for the other. It is not the spiritual work that is for the physical work, but the latter is for the former. This is also how a wise man expresses it: "All men want to live in order to eat, but I eat in order to live." The Divine Assembly has four faces, which look and see on all sides, like Ezekiel's chariot, and it is seen from all directions. That is why the members of this assembly must behave in a manner worthy of it and listen to what Our Lord says: Seek first the kingdom of God and His righteousness, and all these things will be given to you as well. Our business is spiritual; our work is in heaven, says the blessed Paul, from where we await our vivifier and our Lord Jesus Christ, who will transform our vile body to be like his glorious body. We do not run aimlessly like those who beat the air; we do not work by chance, but with the great hope of acquiring spiritual knowledge. Therefore, we must above all love work, love one another, and give our masters the respect they deserve, so that they too, with pleasure and good will, may treat us according to our weakness. If those who engage in worldly circus games before earthly kings deprive themselves, as St. Paul says, of anything that may hinder their profession in order to gain worldly honor, how much more should we abstain from anything contrary to our profession? Therefore, the Apostle advises us to conduct ourselves wisely towards those outside, redeeming the time, and always seasoning our speech with grace as with salt. If those prone to anger and wickedness, once chosen by earthly kings for any task, abstain from their first habits and become gentle and docile, all the more," we must act in the same way. If someone who is invited to enter the king's palace to partake of the food makes every effort to be attentive to his appearance that day, lest he be seen disorderly and be put out, then all the more reason we, who are invited to the heavenly wedding feast, should adorn our souls with virtues worthy of this celebration, lest Our Lord say to us: 'My friend, how did you come in here without a wedding garment?' May God forbid that the dishonor stops there! But no; for he adds: 'Bind him hand and foot, take him away, and cast him into outer darkness.' May God grant that this be temporary! But no; for he continues: 'There will be weeping and gnashing of teeth.' To avoid this punishment, let us apply ourselves to work according to the rules of our teaching, aligning our actions with our instruction: 'Let your light so shine before men, that they may see your good works and glorify your Father who is in heaven.' Remove the evil one from among you; do not associate with him, lest he be confounded; crucify yourself to the world; put off the old man with his works, and put on the new man, who is renewed in knowledge after the image.

Glory and respect be given to Him, to His Father, and to the Holy Spirit throughout all ages. End of 'the Cause of the foundation of the Schools'.

Glory to God and forgiveness of sins to the sinner Thomas. Amen.

REASON FOR THE FOUNDING OF THE SCHOOL

The Scriptorium Project is the work of a small group of lay people of various apostolic churches who are interested in the preservation, transmission, and translation of the works of the early and medieval church. Our efforts are to make the works of the church fathers accessible to anyone who might have an interest in Christian antiquities and the theological, philosophical, and moral writings that have become the bedrock of Western Civilization.

To-date, our releases have pulled from the Greek, Syriac, Georgian, Latin, Celtic, Ethiopian, and Coptic traditions of Christianity, and have been pulled from sundry local traditions and languages.

REASON FOR THE FOUNDING OF THE SCHOOL

REASON FOR THE FOUNDING OF THE SCHOOL